A Changed MIND
=
A Changed LIFE

CHANGE
*C*orrecting *H*abits *A*s *N*eeded for *G*rowth & *E*xcellence

Rachel Spiller Riles

Copyright © 2013 Rachel Spiller Riles

All rights reserved. No portion of this book may be reproduced, stored in a retrieval system, or transmitted in any form or by any means—electronic, mechanical, photocopy, recording, scanning, or other—except for brief quotations in critical reviews or articles, without the prior written permission of the publisher.

Cover Design: Be Excellent Design

ISBN: 0-9856478-1-7
ISBN-13: 978-0-9856478-1-0

S & R Publishing
Houston, Texas
713.364.8440
http://www.rachelspillerriles.com/achangedmind

DEDICATION

This book is dedicated to all who find it challenging to change that which we possess the power to change but never seem to reach a breakthrough!

Table of Contents

Foreword ii

PREFACE 4

Starting Where You Are 7

Introduction 8

The Principles of Change 28

Principle 1: Recognizing the Need for Change 29

Principle 2: Embracing the Process of Change 38

Principle 3: Creating a Culture for Change 49

A Mind-Set for Change 58

Sample Action Plan 91

Action Plan 92

Bibliography 93

ACKNOWLEDGMENTS

Had it not been for the Love of God this book would not be possible. I love the life I am living.

A special thank you to my husband of 31 years, Melvin, for always supporting me.

To my mother, Ruby Spiller, thank you for the biblical foundation you and dad instilled in all of us and for teaching us Proverbs 3:5-6 (Trust in the Lord with all thine heart, and lean not unto thine own understanding; In all thy ways acknowledge him, and he shall direct thy paths.).

To my family: my children, grandchildren, sisters and their husbands, my brother and his wife, thank you.

To Phyllis, Lisa, Tamara, and Toni thank you for your guidance, suggestions, and support!

To Kristena and Cheryl thank you so much for the Video Promo and assisting me with the cover design respectively.

To all my Facebook friends, thank you for the support during this process.

***

__I changed my mind to change my behavior to change my life!__

Foreword

Knowing Rachel as I do, she has dedicated her life to making people better at the expense of her time, effort and energy. This book is a direct result of her passion. Her testimonial states, "I changed my mind to change a behavior that changed my life," is not her speaking about herself but is actually a slogan that she wants her readers to adopt so they too can experience the benefits of a changed life.

This book revolutionizes one perspective on life, in that you discover within each chapter that you are the main ingredient to your success. It is a true statement that we all suffer with unwanted character flaws or unwanted behavioral patterns but not many of us know how to reform ourselves in order to get rid of these personality quirks.

In this book "A Changed Mind = A Changed Life," Rachel Riles has wittingly put together methods that will empower its reader to facilitate in their character so that the positive man within can surface without. She states and I quote, "My desire to change becomes reality when I purposely plan and pursue practices that produce positive results." When you read this book get ready to change your life by changing your behavior from your changed mind.

Dr. Raphael Nicholas Spiller, Th.D

My desire to change becomes reality when I purposely plan and pursue practices that produce positive results!

PREFACE

CHANGE is a universal concept, however, individual perception of change is not. For this reason, the way an individual processes change determines the level of growth or success he or she experiences. This guide explains how using your learning style can assist in changing undesired behaviors or habits.

First let me introduce myself by way of my struggle to change.

In early 1989, I weighed approximately 170 pounds, much more than I had ever weighed. I was an emotional wreck. I stressed over the weight gain and loss of employment. For me, stressing was my excuse to eat. This binge lasted for about six months.
In late July of the same year, I decided to change my appearance. Starting with my hair, I drastically underwent a color change from black to a "burnt orange." Next, I joined "Bally's President and First Lady Health and Fitness Club." I was determined to change who and what I had become. I was motivated to change (temporarily); I created a work-out schedule and changed my diet. My workout included running, lifting weights, playing tennis or any activity that burned calories. My new "DIET" consisted of foods that were low in calories but were not healthy. By year's end, I was down to about 137 pounds. Temporarily losing the weight, building muscles in my arms and legs, and dropping from a size 12 to a size 6 was more than I could have imagined. It was a

very exciting time for me. There was no better feeling than sporting my high school figure, feeling really good about myself, and seeing images of the new person I had become. It was a time of CHANGE for me. That feeling soon began to wither when I found out I was pregnant and began the weight gain. Nine months and 27 pounds later, I gave birth to my son (that was a joy).

For the next 23 years, my weight fluctuated between 180 and 192 pounds. I had become someone unknown to me. My lifestyle had become comfortable. I was content eating whatever I desired without the thought of consequences. Shopping for clothes with "extra"(2x) material and garments associated with mathematics (plus, 16 or 20) was very depressing.

To add fuel to the fire, in 2009, I was diagnosed with Type II Diabetes. Battling two high risk diseases, hypertension and diabetes was certainly a challenge I was not ready to tackle. On one occasion I recall my physician saying "all you have to do is eat right and exercise and we can possibly reduce the medication or even discontinue it altogether." There was a glimmer of hope.

I began contemplating the change I would have to make. First, I considered hypertension the priority issue. It was difficult recognizing the behavior I needed to change. Changing behaviors can be challenging, even more so when the undesired behavior or habit is incorrectly identified. For example, when I was first diagnosed with hypertension, I mistakenly believed "not adding salt to my cooked meals" was the answer to lowering my sodium intake; however, an increased sodium intake very seldom comes from adding table-salt. High sodium levels also come from foods that are processed, canned, and packed for long shelf-life. The behavior I needed to change was eating foods with a "high sodium content."

Change requires a different mind-set. In December, 2012, some decisions had to be made if I no longer wanted to take medication. If I wanted to live longer as a result of my decisions, I had to make a change. I had to internalize the meaning of the change I sought. How could I live a healthy life: mind, body, and spirit? Once I recognized that behavioral changes were a direct result of a changed mind, a plan to change my thinking was inevitable. I knew what had to be done.

In the words of Aristotle, "we are what we repeatedly do. Excellence then is not an act, but a habit." I needed to create new habits.

"My desire to change only becomes reality when I purposely plan and pursue practices that produce positive results."

Starting Where You Are

One "true" look in the mirror resulted in a step in the right direction. It wasn't the literal view that concerned me. This time, I saw with my mind and not with my eyes. I was tired of going on diets. My struggle to lose weight had become so burdensome until I wanted to just give up on the idea of "being small" again.

What was I to do? My family didn't complain nor did any of my friends. I had become tolerant of being "overweight." I was simply living to eat. My eating habits had become a standard of living. More importantly, I had no burning desire to change.

Not until December 2012 did I consider a change was necessary. If I lived beyond the age of 60, what kind of lifestyle would I have? I began to imagine the challenges others faced with the same medical issues. The picture was gruesome and unbecoming of one who once was a very athletic and health conscious individual.

As you began to consider the challenges you face today, whether health related or not, remember it is very important to the process of change that you are realistic in your thinking. Committing to unrealistic change will result in perpetually undesired outcomes.

Introduction

This book provides a platform for the discussion of change and offers three suggested principles on changing undesired behaviors/habits for growth and excellence.

- **Understanding your learning style** – explains the three basic learning styles and the perspective of learning theorists on learning
- **Defining Change** – Correcting Habits As Needed for Growth & Excellence
- **The Principles of Change**
    - **Principle 1** – Recognizing the Need for Change – focuses on conducting a Needs Assessment, identifying your learning styles and how to identify undesired behaviors
    - **Principle 2** – Embracing the Process of Change – focuses on the process of change, and behaviors that should be adopted to promote change
    - **Principle 3** – Creating a Culture for Change – focuses on establishing an environment conducive for the change you desire
- **A Mind-Set for Change** –thinking with a purpose for 30 days. You are encouraged to reflect on each daily quote

<u>**Purposed Thinking**</u> *You are the change you have been waiting for.*

Understanding Your Learning Style

Using Your Style Of Learning To Help Change Undesired Behaviors

Some learning theorists suggest behaviors are learned based on social interactions, environmental stimuli, and individual experiences.

In this book, I have chosen to share how change can occur utilizing your learning style. While others may use different techniques, I recognize that change is a process and requires more than just a book of words. The quotes, commentary, scriptures and the breakdown of learning styles in this book are designed to successfully assist anyone with changing undesired behaviors or habits.

What is meant by learning styles? According to Seller (2011), "learning styles can be defined as the way each person concentrates on, processes, internalizes, and retains new and difficult academic information" (p.133) When we consider how a person learns, the understanding of how a behavior is formed should be clearer. In order for a behavior to be learned, one must engage in the process of learning. This holds true when changing a behavior as well.

Adults as well as children establish foundations for learning, whether that foundation is parent-based or as a result of life experiences.

Psychologist Erik Erikson, who's theory of psychosocial development suggest that learning occurs in stages. If a stage is managed unsatisfactorily, evidence will manifest later in development. According to Kendra Cherry (2013), noted author and educator, "in each stage, Erikson believed people experience a conflict that serves as a turning point in development. In Erikson's view, these conflicts are centered on either developing a psychological quality or failing to develop that quality. During these times, the potential for personal growth is high, but so is the potential for failure." When we consider our present behaviors, the question to explore is whether or not we have manifestations of unmanaged psychosocial learning stages.

Another psychological perspective is that of John B. Watson, the father of Behaviorism. Watson, unlike Erikson, believed behaviors were a result of some type of stimuli. When presented with a stimulus, a particular behavior was elicited, known as conditioned response. This evidence supports the theory of learned behavior.

Consider your behaviors. Do you find yourself responding to conditioned or unconditioned (food) stimuli?

When a response or behavior is repeated based on a conditioned or unconditioned stimulus, the learned response is said to be conditioned or unconditioned. Regardless of the outcome, Behaviorists believe the behavior or habit is learned. Do you have any conditioned responses? Who or what is controlling your behavior? Whether behaviors are conditioned or not, when they are undesired and you want to change them, the process of change is the same. You must decide if the behavior or habit is within your power to change. If it is, then commit to actions necessary to develop new behaviors or habits to replace those undesired ones.

Most people are unaware of their learning style. Take a moment and consider your style of learning. Do you learn best by hearing, reading, or hands-on (actively participating)? Some individuals possess more than one style of learning. Whatever the style, embrace it, perfect it, and use it to change undesired behaviors.

To reach a break-through, each chapter of this book helped me design and implement a Plan of Action. More importantly than any suggestive information this book can offer, being convinced change is necessary and committed to following through is essentially the attitude required to see undesired behaviors changed.

Using Critical Thinking Skills to Change Behaviors

As an educator, I try and create the most optimal learning environment for students to learn. Not only is it important to utilize your learning style to create change, but combining the learning style with levels of thinking takes behavior change to another level.

Purposed thinking is critical thinking.

Bloom's Taxonomy

For the purpose of learning how to change, let's look at what educators have adopted as ways to build critical thinking. In 1956, Dr. Benjamin Bloom published six levels of thinking known as Bloom's Taxonomy. These levels of thinking suggest that learning can be observed at the lowest form, Knowledge and pass through to the highest level, Evaluation.

In the 1990's a former student of Dr. Bloom's revised the original taxonomy into what is now called "Revised Bloom's." The Revised Bloom's Taxonomy suggests "creating" is the highest level of thinking.

Thinking is to learning as breathing is to living. However, with learning, the level of your thinking determines your intelligence. Changing undesired behaviors is simply "learning new" ones. The level of thinking applied to learning the new behavior requires more than just memorization. In order to change unwanted behaviors to desired ones, one should be able to think critically! Understanding the role critical thinking plays in learning is important to changing undesired behaviors or habits. According to the Revised Bloom's, when we change unproductive habits into new and fruitful ones, we employ critical thinking. Changing undesired behaviors requires new thinking. Think creatively!

In this book, I refer to three principles of change as *R.E.C.(pronounced "wreck")*:

- **R**ecognizing the need for change,
- **E**mbracing the process of change, and
- **C**reating a culture for change.

Notice the principles are designed to move an individual through the process of change by applying the theory of critical thinking. The first principle simply requires a lower level of thinking. When considering changing habits or behaviors, an individual must **RECOGNIZE** the need for change. The second principle requires more in-depth thinking, in that you must **EMBRACE** the process of change. This is simply done by applying action to a set of specified goals. Finally, the third principle requires you to **CREATE** a culture for change. To ensure old habits do not resurface, one must develop new standards for living with new behaviors or habits.

In the next section, we discuss the meaning of change. As you engage in the thought of change, consider your way of thinking:

- How does change occur?
- What is your perception of change?

- How will changing an unwanted habit affect your lifestyle?

Defining Change

CHANGE IS ABOUT YOU...

You are the single most important person in your quest for change ~
Rachel Spiller Riles

Recognizing the truth is the first step in the process of change. Change is more than stating you want to change. One of the most common desires to change comes at the beginning of each year in the form of a New Year's Resolution. We make promises to change a particular behavior but within a couple of months, we are back to our old habits.

Why is it so difficult for people to change behaviors?

Harvard Women's Health Watch suggests, "one problem may be that we're motivated too often by a sense of guilt, fear, or regret. Experts who study behavior change agree that long-lasting change is most likely when it's self-motivated and rooted in positive thinking."(2007)

Changing behaviors is the sole responsibility of the individual. The desire alone is not enough for successful change to take place. You must recognize that you are the single most important person in your quest for change!

As you consider your change in behavior, understand that practicing a particular behavior or habit increases the likelihood of mastering that behavior or habit. Take my health for example. I was diagnosed with hypertension around age 20. I was not particularly overweight and doctors were unable to pinpoint specific contributing factors. Since there were no symptoms, I did not place significant emphasis on corrective measures. Research has shown most people do not change their bad habits even when faced with health challenges. Instead, they continue with the negative behavior.

If we understand that change can only occur when we make a conscious decision to face facts about undesired behavior, then we must acknowledge change is a process.

CHANGE IS LIFE

You can't change your life unless you change your behavior, and you can't change your behavior unless you change your mind.
~ Rachel Spiller Riles

Changing behaviors is like trying on clothes or shoes too small. It is a challenge getting in and out. When you're looking for different results or outcomes but continue with the same behavior, it is then that you must decide whether or not to alter the current behavior or remain the same. Always remember, outcomes only change when there is a change in behavior.

Mental variants or changes pose the most challenge when planning to change a behavior. I refer to this as *mental incarceration: when you knowingly lock your mind around negative situations and circumstances and allow your actions to be controlled by such.* Learn to accept some situations and circumstances and discount others. Because we do not possess the power to change everything in our lives, it is important to focus on that which we have control over.

Research on early brain development supports the idea that learning occurs prior to birth. Have you ever wondered if some of your early behaviors stem from prenatal learning?

As you prepare for CHANGE, consider the following:

Food for Thought

- Are you ready to accept the change that is necessary?
- Do you find yourself giving in to your weaknesses or challenges?
- Has someone told you something needs to change?
- Have you tried changing before?
- Do you have the power to change what needs to be changed?

Positive thoughts produce powerful images of the possibilities that can be achieved with persistence and practice.

~ Rachel Spiller Riles

Purposed Thinking The mindset we adopt is essential to the success of changing undesired behaviors. As you think purposefully about productive behaviors, give consideration to your perception of CHANGE. You can only change that which you believe can be changed.

CHANGE IS LIBERTY

When you procrastinate, you hold hostage the keys to your success! ~ Rachel Spiller Riles

Change is...

- not conforming to the world view but renewing the mind daily with truth,
- denying the principles of procrastination,
- speaking truth to negative propaganda, be it friend or foe,
- FREEDOM!

Today is the day you start something new. Do not worry about how you are going to do it, just decree and declare you are going to do IT!

If you have desired to accomplish something but other "stuff" keeps getting in the way then examine yourself to make sure you are not simply putting "it" off. My life is filled with "starting this and starting that" but never actually completing any of it. Vowing to end the relationship I had with procrastination was a struggle. However, I recognized my success depended on my thought process. Far too often I would conjure up fascinating ideas only to let them die in my imagination. Another or better idea seemed to always supersede the last one.

While writing this book, I set a goal to complete the first draft in one month. I was sure it would get done because I had all the information needed to complete it. However, the relationship I had developed with procrastination was stronger than my desire to succeed. Once I developed an understanding of how procrastination affected progress, I made a conscious decision to change my thought process.

Procrastination vs. Rachel Spiller Riles

The "Papers" have been signed! Today is the day you divorce yourself from procrastination. You've allowed this relationship to sabotage your dreams and desires... continued involvement jeopardizes your destiny.

After acknowledging the behavior, I identified specifics about when procrastination showed up, where it showed up, and why it showed up. Procrastination and I were a team. Wherever I went, it followed. A note of clarification is necessary here. Things got accomplished and I did progress in many of my life endeavors. It just took longer. For example, my first college degree was completed in fifteen years as oppose to four or five years. I received my Master's degree in nine years whereas most people finish in two to four years. My success was held hostage by the relationship I shared with procrastination.

You have waited too long to fulfill your dreams. You developed unproductive relationships that have kept you from succeeding. Excuses, excuses, excuses! But no longer will you stay a captive. You deserve better, you can achieve more because you were created to succeed.

Whatever your Spiritual convictions, use them. For me, I recognized it was time to allow God to position me to receive his plans for my life.

Expect the unexpected, but do not allow the unknown to create fear where confidence should reside.

Purposed Thinking It is time for you to recognize your UNIQUENESS, your GIFTEDNESS, and your POTENTIAL! Today is the day you start allowing your words to dictate your SUCCESS!

CHANGE IS ACTION

Your willingness to change can be measured by the success of your actions! ~ Rachel Spiller Riles

Be different!

The world tries to dictate how we live our lives by using social media, environmental influences, and even educational issues to aid in forming our belief and value systems. Change is more challenging when you conform to societal expectations. We are all uniquely created and possess a set of innate qualities that are designed to "fashion" each of us into our destined being. When we allow opinions of others to define us we become replicas of them.

When we consistently perform a specific action, we grow more comfortable and confident in continuing to repeat that action. Regardless of the behavior, positive or negative, if you continue to exercise that behavior, you form a habit.
Therefore, a behavior change requires that you **DO** something differently in order to obtain different results.

Purposed Thinking *"The world as we have created it is a process of our thinking. It cannot be changed without changing our thinking."* ~ Albert Einstein

CHANGE IS VISION

See yourself as a product of your future and not as a casualty of your past! ~ Rachel Spiller Riles

Change is recognizing that your past is neither your present nor your future! No matter what you have done in your past, the sky is the limit to what you can achieve if you believe in yourself.

If your past experiences keep you from seeing future possibilities then allow your past to take a permanent vacation. If the change you seek requires new scenery, by all means, move some things, replace some people, or travel to different places. Friends and family have a unique way of spotlighting your past once you have made a conscious decision to change. Nonetheless, allow them to witness the new you.

Remember, always treat a negative with a positive. A behavior is an action learned; therefore, let every new behavior result from a purposed-informed decision.

The power to change the necessary lies within your mental capacity; believing in that power, indicates your past can no longer dictate your future response.

Purposed Thinking If yesterday does not contribute to the success of your tomorrow, then recognize that the Change you seek lies in today's decisions. Your future depends on it.

The Principles of Change

➢ Recognizing the need for change

➢ Embracing the process of change

➢ Creating a culture for change

Principle 1: Recognizing the Need for Change

RECOGNIZING THE MENTAL PICTURE

The obvious is but a mental picture waiting for you to create a masterpiece or not; the choice is yours!
~ Rachel Spiller Riles

Change is necessary when your existing behavior does not contribute to the positive growth and development of your self-image, your self-actualization or your self-efficacy.

Because change is a process, it is imperative that a 'Needs Assessment' be conducted.

Focus on behaviors you have the power to change. Although we may have different behaviors we wish to modify, the same approach toward identifying the needed change is the same. I recall how my health became more challenging as I gained weight. The process of change could not begin because I had not fully and completely recognized the contributing behavioral factors responsible for my health challenges.

When the obvious is revealed, either through self-reflection or by some other method, do not hesitate to consider the possibility of change. Behaviors are like extensions of our extremities. They are always with us, whether we intentionally use them or not. As they impress upon our mental framework, we must acknowledge their existence and be willing to recreate, reprogram, or recapture new images.

I recognized where my consistent *failures* originated. They were present in everything I attempted to accomplish. Finally, I acknowledged my limitations and made a conscious decision to change that which I had control over.

What was the *obvious*? For me, it was about restructuring my eating habits and building confidence in my abilities. It was about changing what I fed my mind, body, and spirit.

The mental pictures we create of ourselves can be tailored to resemble the masterpiece awaiting to be formed. It is our decision to envision our future. I choose to acknowledge my present and use my past as a springboard to my future.

Consider the quote "the obvious is but a mental picture waiting for you to create a masterpiece or not; the choice is yours," then compare how you see yourself now with what you would like to see in the future.

_____
_____
_____
_____
_____
_____
_____

Successful businessman Jim Rohn suggests, "you must take personal responsibility. You cannot change the circumstances, the seasons, or the wind, but you can change yourself. That is something you have charge of."

We are responsible for the successful change we desire. Others can never be the reason for our failure to succeed. The decisions we make, whether they involve people, places or things, directly impacts our lives.

What in your past has prevented you from being successful in the change you now seek? Explain below.

(Example: My decision to eat late at night has contributed to my weight gain; my decision to allow others to discourage me from pursing my goals has prevented me from accomplishing my goals)

_____
_____
_____
_____
_____
_____
_____
_____

RECOGNIZING THE WISDOM OF CHANGE

The difference between knowledge and ignorance is the amount you would have saved had you known!
~ Rachel Spiller Riles

Feeding the mind for success requires purposeful input, not haphazardly selected but purposed to produce. The need for change occurs when your daily routine leaves out the development of your thought process.

One of my favorite writers, John Maxwell (2009), suggests "those who embrace good thinking as a lifestyle understand the relationship between their level of thinking and their level of progress."

Ignorance is costly. Consider having knowledge of an upcoming sale on your favorite items. You attend the sale and save a considerable amount. Quite naturally you are elated. Now contrast that without the knowledge of the sale. How much more would you have spent?

Recently my husband and I attended a tax appraisal hearing for the first time. We did not know what to expect. To get more information about the hearing I questioned friends and family members. Many of them instructed me to take pictures, while an appraisal employee suggested researching the sold homes in my area that were similar to my home.

Once we arrived, the process was explained. We would be given an opportunity to present our case and then offer final comments after an appraisal district representative presented on behalf of the district. Still a little apprehensive about the procedure, I began to present photos of our home, spoke about the major repairs needed and offered evidence of recently sold properties. The district's representative began to present less than favorable evidence against our argument. We presented final comments and the deliberation (none) began. The decision was unanimous.

We were informed of the final decision only to be disappointed about the increase in property taxes. The independent panel suggested we do our "homework" next time. We should have provided color photos, estimates of repairs, photos of damaged property and more sold properties.

At that moment I realized "the difference between knowledge and ignorance was $30,000, the amount I could have saved had I known."

The importance of knowledge is not to be able to say you have it, but to use it to make a difference. Understanding undesired behaviors and the consequences that result, helps build a valuable knowledge-base necessary for critical thinking; therefore, when you consider the decisions you must make, ask yourself how much you know about what you are getting ready to decide on. Rethink your decision if you are making it without the necessary information to choose wisely. Ignorance is simply, not knowing. But not knowing can be the difference between poverty and wealth.

Recognizing the need for change is not only the first principle of change, it is the most important of the three. For it is at this level where you begin the thinking process. Remember, change is a process and so is your thinking. Compare it to building a house. You must first lay the foundation before you build the frame.

Changing undesired behaviors requires an understanding of how the behavior affects our lives and a willingness to take corrective action, even if that action is painful.

Purposed Thinking I believe God gives wisdom…As you get knowledge also get an understanding…according to the Bible, that is wisdom. Do not allow yourself to be controlled by the unproductive and unhealthy speech and actions of those who cannot give life or liberty.

RECOGNIZING THE POWER OF YOUR WORDS

You are only as powerful as the words you speak.
~ Rachel Spiller Riles

I was thinking the other day about the importance of words and the difference between telling and showing. A startling truth, arose, "talk is cheap," unless the words spoken are ACTIVE.

When we are faced with the challenge of changing behaviors, what we speak and what we are silent about becomes relative to successful change. Quite often words are spoken to encourage, ridicule, degrade, or for no apparent reason at all. I want my words to mean something. No longer will I speak without thinking. No longer will I accept what others say without "considering" what is being said. Recognizing the need for change requires one to think first, then, speak with substance. Words represent the POWER needed to jumpstart the "vehicle of change." The substance of what you say provides the FUEL. Whatever is being said to you, about you, or from you, be sure and weigh it first. Ask yourself these questions, "is it relevant to my present circumstance", "what authority does the messenger have over the information;" and "how important will the information be to me in six months?"

According to scripture, "death and life are in the power of the tongue." (KJV – Proverbs 18:21) Learn to speak with authority over that which you have the power to change. Let your mind "speak" your success! Let your words bring into existence what your thoughts have already purposed in your heart!

Your words are merely thoughts of your being. Therefore declare:

- I am successful
- I am full of ideas
- I am a finisher
- I am light in a dark room
- I am a product of my thinking!

Purposed Thinking – You are only as powerful as the words you speak.

Principle 2: Embracing the Process of Change

EMBRACING THE PROCESS OF CHANGE

My desire to change becomes reality when I purposely plan and pursue practices that produce positive results.
~ Rachel Spiller Riles

I possess the power to change my behaviors. My strong belief in the power to change is attributed to the relationship I enjoy with the "life-giver KING, Jesus." I would be negligent in my thinking if I did not acknowledge how the "Word of God" gives me inner power, peace and poise.

Before you begin to reduce this message to some "religious" anecdote, take inventory of your own personal beliefs and spirituality. If you find a *higher power*, embrace the benefits of that relationship and allow IT to bring you to a place of conviction and contemplation in order to change.

When I consider the attitude of Christ, I recognize how He operated successfully as He embraced the power He was given. The POWER manifested as He operated according to God's purpose, principles and plan for His life. Because I believe I am HIS, He resides in me along with the power I need to operate fully in my life's purpose!

"Greater is He who is in you, than he who is in the world!"
(I John 4:4b KJV)

Embracing the process of change means you accept that which you have no power to change.

Today is the day you stop trying to change the attitude and behaviors of others but know that you are the one who controls how you respond to their actions.

When I resolved in my mind that I was not the "4th part of the Trinity," I then allowed God to reveal to me what I needed to focus on. I hesitantly accepted some obvious truths about my lifestyle. Why did it take so long? Oft times we are not moved to see ourselves; however, embracing change requires us to be honest and open-minded.

Consider your current practices to change an undesired behavior. What do you *purposely* do to avoid the behavior?

1. _____
_____
_____
_____
_____

Procrastination has a way of delaying progress. It was one of the challenges I hesitantly admitted. Nevertheless, if I was going to succeed, I needed to embrace the process to change from procrastination to active participation.

Your learning style is valuable to the successful implementation of "Embracing the Process of Change."

If you are:
- ❖ An Auditory Learner - researchers say you tend to learn through talking and listening to music; you are distracted by background noise; you memorize by repeating things aloud, and when reading, you whisper the words;

  When learning a new behavior or habit:
   - try listening to audio books, videos, and public presentations;
   - read out loud;
- ❖ A Kinesthetic Learner – According to researchers you remember what was done as oppose to what was said; you tend to rely on that which you can directly do or experience; you speak with your hands and gestures; you bore easily when not actively involved in the process;

  Try learning new behaviors by:
   - acting out the change you want to see
   - creating diagrams or posters of what you would like to see changed
   - use computer software to create presentations about your change
   - use a cell phone camera to take pictures of what you want to see changed;
   - remember this style of learning enjoys being part of the action.
- ❖ A Visual Learner – you find it easier to learn new things by viewing them, you interpret directions by viewing diagrams and maps as oppose to hearing them;

  Try enhancing your learning by:
   - translating words and ideas into symbols, pictures and diagrams

- using to-do lists, assignment logs and written notes (which also benefits kinesthetic learners)

*Consider your learning style, then list ways you can use it to help you embrace the process of change. Remember, embracing the process of change begins with applying new strategies or new thinking to the new habit/behavior.

_____
_____
_____
_____
_____
_____
_____

Purposed Thinking – Change comes to those who ponder to change, plan to change, and then practice to change! Embrace CHANGE!

EMBRACING THE IMAGINATION

"See with your mind and not with your eyes!"
~ Rachel Spiller Riles

The mind is a very powerful device. It is equipped with connecting devices that have functions not fully known to man. Philosophers suggest that a man ceases to exist when he can no longer think. According to the Holy Bible, "so a man thinketh in his heart, so is he" (Proverbs 23:7 KJV). The interpretation here suggests that the "heart" and "mind" are one. Because we understand that a man thinks with his mind, we can conclude that our thoughts reveal who we are mentally, emotionally, and spiritually.

As an educator, I recognize the importance of understanding the role the imagination plays in learning. Mental vision captures life's infinite possibilities.

When we consider changing a particular behavior, we must first identify the specifics of the behavior. Most often, we focus on the obvious. For example, when I considered my weight, I would concentrate on what the scale revealed instead of the fact that my diet consisted of foods that promoted weight gain.

Creating a mental picture of the change you seek is imperative to a successful "mind change." You must first "think" the "change" before you can "see" the change. Thinking the change helps internalize it. Become "one" with the change you desire.

The question now is how do you create a "mental picture" of the change you seek? First, create the thought. Then create action to support the thought. For example, if you want to lose weight, picture the weight loss. Then develop an action plan to DO something different that will impact your lifestyle. It is not enough just to change your eating habits. The operative word is "do." Remember, the thought comes before the action. If you find it difficult to create mental pictures, then the change you seek may need reevaluating.

Ask the question, "Can I visualize the change I seek? Yes or No (If not, rethink the change).

Identify the behavior you must change in order for the mental picture to become a reality. In the words of Albert Einstein, "we cannot solve our problems with the same thinking we used when we created them."

What behavior do you desire to change? Be specific and realistic with the description of your change. Modifying behaviors can only be achieved when you are clear and concise about the undesired behavior.

Perhaps you are interested in weight loss. Most people who are trying to lose weight usually start by stating what they will do rather than what they are no longer going to do. Undesired behaviors cannot be undone simply by ignoring them. A conscious decision to replace the behavior/habit with a desired one is necessary.

For example, if drinking soft drinks is a problem, you may want to say something like *"I will stop drinking 6 sodas a day and start drinking eight 8-ounce glasses of water every day." ***See yourself (mental picture)** drinking 64 ounces of water a day. Picture yourself without a bottle of soda. Whatever the issue, remember to see with your mind and not with your eyes.

Try listing three behaviors you would like to change. Write the behavior as it is today, followed by what you perceive the truth to become. (See example above*)

1. _____
2. _____
3. _____

"Incredible change happens in your life when you decide to take control of what you do have power over instead of craving control over what you don't." ~ *Steve Maraboli*

Purposed Thinking – If you can imagine it, you can change it!

EMBRACING TIME

Time is a limited but valuable commodity; time is maximized when time is ordered; your lack of success with change is an indication of how you allocate time! Use your time wisely!
~ Rachel Spiller Riles

There is no pause in time. If time is valuable then why must I be patient? When I consider the meaning of time, I am assured of one thing and that is, time passes.

We now understand that changing undesired behaviors is a process that requires time. When embracing the process of change, we must reverence time. Time passed is time unrecoverable; therefore, our time should be allocated wisely. If I'm assigned a task that requires time management and I don't fully commit to the task, I will allow time to escape, producing an unfinished task. .

When changing undesired behaviors, remember time is your friend and biggest supporter. If you mismanage or treat time unfairly, you will quickly discover a valuable lesson: **time can also be your greatest enemy**.

Planning for change is crucial to its success. How do you maximize your time? Embracing time means reflecting on how you allocate time; it means prioritizing; it means saying "no" when necessary. What activity, person, or place receives most of your time? If the answer to that question contributes to you reaching the next level then continue on that path. However, if you find yourself complaining about not having enough time to complete tasks, reevaluate your *time schedule*.

Wherever you find solace, get there and spend quality time examining your current understanding and mastery of time management. You may find, as I did, that most of your set-backs or temporary delays are a result of how you structure time.

How would reallocating your time contribute to your success?

_____

_____

_____

_____

_____

Purposed Thinking   *Idleness produces a harvest of wasted time!*

Principle 3: Creating a Culture for Change

YOUR CHARACTER

What is the relationship between change and character? I was reading an article about the famous baseball player, Alex Rodriguez. He touts an impressive list of stats among major league baseball players. His hometown supporters as well as others shell out thousands of dollars on "A-Rod" memorabilia. However, according to news reports, a shadow of doubt has been cast upon his impressive baseball career because of reports of steroid use. Rodriguez, however, still enjoys an overwhelming support from fans and former mayor of New York, Rudy Giuliani.

It goes without question having a celebratory reputation sometimes excuses misbehavior. Although controlling the behavior of others is highly unlikely, we can set standards for ourselves and demonstrate to others what character should look like.

Establishing a culture for change, regarding undesired behaviors, requires one to evaluate current behaviors. It is my character that determines whether or not change is possible. If I find myself in the company of people that do not "fit" in my "circle of change" the likelihood of me conforming to the behaviors of the group increases.

When your character matches positive behavior, the combination produces limitless possibilities. Take for example George C. Bolt. He managed the prestigious Bellevue Hotel in Philadelphia in the late eighteen hundreds. One evening a couple arrived at the Bellevue only to be met with a "no vacancy" response. However, Mr. Bolt agreed to allow the couple to occupy his family's suite for the night. Such a gesture was a testament to his character. How many hotel managers would be willing to give up their personal living quarters for a couple in search of a room for the night?

The significance of the story lies in the manager's character. I believe if Mr. Bolt did not have a spirit of *service,* the couple may have had to look elsewhere for accommodations. As the story continues, the husband and wife were the famous Waldorf's of the Hotel Waldorf-Astoria in New York. Because of his character and generosity, and at the request of Mr. Waldorf, Mr. Bolt became the manager of the Waldorf.

Undesired behaviors demonstrate our character and can open or close doors of opportunity. Can you identify any current behavior or habit that may place you at a disadvantage of succeeding in any area of your life?

As you consider SUCCESS, keep in mind that it is your character at risk; therefore, think before you speak or act.

As you develop winning character traits, remember to be **reflective**. I sometimes take a "self-identification" check. Who knows you better than you? It is important to be honest about the perceptions others have of you, the behaviors that are requiring more time but are less productive, and your own strengths and weaknesses.

I admire the President of the United States, Barak Obama, for one important quality, his character. I may not agree with his political stance on some issues, nevertheless, his demonstration of calm in the midst of a storm is worth adopting. He brings new meaning to the phrase "never let them see you sweat." Throughout his 2008 campaign he was subjected to some very disheartening speech. Instead of allowing the actions of others to control his environment, his response was to "live above" what he had no control over.

How do you respond to unwanted comments and criticisms?
_____
_____
_____
_____

Purposed thinking exposes my mind to infinite possibilities and sets in motion the wheels of success!

***<u>Purposed Thinking</u>** When I speak, I give permission to a state of mind that responds to success or defeat!*

YOUR ENVIRONMENT

Creating a culture for change may require the pruning of our surroundings which may include friends and family.

"Your level of intelligence is suggested by the company you keep." ~ Rachel Spiller Riles

Our environment, which includes people, places, and things, directly impacts our view on change. But just how we view change is not enough to create the environment we desire.

"When your emotions for change match your actions for change, then change becomes reality!"
~ Rachel Spiller Riles

When your environment does not contribute to your success, reevaluate your surroundings. Sometimes you have to leave your friends out of your season of change. Research shows the brain reacts to its surroundings. Therefore, if you want to successfully change undesired behaviors, change your environment to resemble the change you seek.

Visual Learners

- **Try displaying pictures of your ideal environment**
- **If possible, relocate your residence or job, etc.**
- **Try meeting new people**

Kinesthetic Learners

- **Change your routine; try doing what you have always done, differently**
- **Enroll in an exercise/weight program**
- **Change your diet**

Auditory Learners

- **Listen to the voice of change for your specific situation**
- **Change your music**
- **Listen to audio books or view videos about change and success**
- **Develop new vocabulary that reflects new thinking**

Purposed Thinking If the results of yesterday's decisions are not today's motivation for success, then let tomorrow's motivation be the result of today's decisions.

YOUR TENACITY

"Success is making IT happen when circumstances say it can't. You WIN!"~ Rachel Spiller Riles

When creating a culture for change, diligence and tenacity are required to persevere. Research shows that when people desire to change negative behaviors, the pressure to succeed sometimes outweighs that desire. We must keep in mind that change comes to those who believe change can be achieved.

Having the tenacity to follow through with your goals for change is great; however, do not allow your quest for change to consume your efforts to the point of not being realistic. Tenacious individuals are driven by the will to succeed. Carl Lewis, world record holder track & field athlete, demonstrated his persistence and determination when others failed to believe anyone could jump a distance of thirty feet. Well, Carl disproved the myths by setting a world record and jumping over 30 feet to win the gold medal. Tenacious individuals who tailor their lifestyles for success find more reasons to celebrate even when the outlook on situations are not as promising. Winners find a way to win, even in the face of adversity. The key to determination is your perception. Your life experiences serve as the framework for your perceived ideas. Therefore, if your experiences limit your perception of success, expose yourself to people, place, things, and ideas that will redefine your frame of reference.

I was reading a Fox News article about a young Latina girl, Olga Custodio, whose life was filled with experiences of traveling the world. She attributes her decisions in life to the exposure her parents provided for her. Her father was a "military man" who traveled across the world with his family.

Traveling with her parents, provided the exposure she needed to convince herself she could one day become a pilot. The odds were against her because of the difficulty in securing a slot in flight training school. However, Olga would not take "**no**" for an answer. She was determined to "get in" and succeed. She was persistent in her pursuit for success.

Whatever change was necessary, she embraced it and persevered. Beating the odds, she became the first Latina US Military pilot.

When you set your mind on being successful, whether changing behaviors or any other challenge, find a way to make it happen. Persistence, patience, practice and prayer are ingredients for successful change.

Creating a culture for change requires one to perceive the desired change, position oneself for change, and practice the process of change.

Purposed Thinking *Your life experiences shape your thoughts, emotions, and actions.*

A Mind-Set for Change

How I think impacts my attitude, which determines my success or failure in every aspect of my life.
~ Rachel Spiller Riles

Noted theologian, author and pastor, Dr. A. Louis Patterson, Jr. explains that growth comes by way of training. Dr. Patterson enlightens us with what I call methods of teaching, "tell to know, teach to show, and train to grow." (n.d.) This perspective certainly explains why many of us may find it difficult to see growth in ourselves. Perhaps we are not engaged in training. When you want to experience growth, consider being trained. Train your spirit, train your mind, and train your body!

For the next 30 days use this section to *Purposely Think* about CHANGE! Record your thoughts about each quote and how you will use the thought to change undesired behaviors.

*C*orrecting *H*abits *A*s *N*eeded for *G*rowth & *E*xcellence

A MIND-SET FOR CHANGE
DAY 1

Change is Correcting Habits As Needed for Growth & Excellence!

_____
_____
_____
_____
_____
_____
_____
_____
_____
_____
_____
_____

A MIND-SET FOR CHANGE
DAY 2

Purposed Thinking is to the mind as water is to the body!

A MIND-SET FOR CHANGE
DAY 3

Never allow the opinions of others to define you; when you do, you become a replica of their thoughts and character… be unique, different, and by all means be YOURSELF!

_____
_____
_____
_____
_____
_____
_____
_____
_____
_____
_____
_____
_____
_____
_____

A MIND-SET FOR CHANGE
DAY 4

Your approach to change reveals your attitude toward success!

A MIND-SET FOR CHANGE
DAY 5

Every day is a new day; but on a journey, it's one step closer to reaching your destination!

_____
_____
_____
_____
_____
_____
_____
_____
_____
_____
_____
_____
_____
_____
_____
_____

A MIND-SET FOR CHANGE
DAY 6

Expect more, aim high and go beyond to reach the next level!

A MIND-SET FOR CHANGE
DAY 7

When you spread yourself too thin, you minimize the full effect of your contribution which then leads to undesired results.

A MIND-SET FOR CHANGE
DAY 8

My advice to others: to occupy space in my mind, advance payment is required. No payment, no vacancy; Keep your opinions!

A MIND-SET FOR CHANGE
DAY 9

Let your prayers be the visual perception (FAITH) of the reality you desire manifested in your present circumstance! For God is omnipresent, omnipotent, and omniscient!

A MIND-SET FOR CHANGE
DAY 10

Finish what you start before you start on something new to insure what you started get's the time and attention needed.

A MIND-SET FOR CHANGE
DAY 11

Change your mind to change your behavior to change your life.

A MIND-SET FOR CHANGE
DAY 12

When you rely on the opinions of others to validate your worth, you constrict the creative vessels of your mind thereby producing mental arrest.

A MIND-SET FOR CHANGE
DAY 13

If I only plan for the "right now", then the "never will be" becomes the future; therefore, I see the "right now" but plan for "what is to become" and believe that the power within me, which is greater than the forces around me, will catapult my plans into existence!

A MIND-SET FOR CHANGE
DAY 14

Your perception of the situation, which is based on a frame of reference shaped by your life experiences, defines your emotions and your responses!

A MIND-SET FOR CHANGE
DAY 15

People can change who you are when you relinquish the power you have over that which you can change yourself!

A MIND-SET FOR CHANGE
DAY 16

Free yourself of mental incarceration by unlocking the inside deadbolt with the key you've always had but never believed you possessed the power to turn it in the right direction!

A MIND-SET FOR CHANGE
DAY 17

I have a choice! I choose to believe what God says about me! Therefore, I reprogram my "hard drive" every time I hear words spoken contrary to God's word concerning me! "you can't do that" - REPROGRAM..."that's never been done before" - REPROGRAM..."you don't have the money" - REPROGRAM!

A MIND-SET FOR CHANGE
DAY 18

Success and failure have "u" in common…the decisions you make determine whether you succeed or fail.

A MIND-SET FOR CHANGE
DAY 19

Don't delay; move with dispatch; your change comes when your emotions match your actions!

A MIND-SET FOR CHANGE
DAY 20

Your mind is the computer, your mouth is the printer...what you print is a reflection of your input! THINK BIG!

A MIND-SET FOR CHANGE
DAY 21

You are a product of your thinking!

A MIND-SET FOR CHANGE
DAY 22

Let the decisions you make today be the History that repeats itself tomorrow!

A MIND-SET FOR CHANGE
DAY 23

The power to change resides within; however, if you do not connect to it you remain as an automobile without an engine: parked

A MIND-SET FOR CHANGE
DAY 24

Be convinced of the change you desire and committed to the process to achieve it!

___

A MIND-SET FOR CHANGE
DAY 25

Time is of no value when life has no purpose.

A MIND-SET FOR CHANGE
DAY 26

If knowing your purpose in life propels you to your destination; then not knowing suggests an unfulfilled life; what is your purpose?

_____

_____

_____

_____

_____

_____

_____

_____

_____

_____

_____

_____

_____

A MIND-SET FOR CHANGE
DAY 27

Your heart reveals your thoughts; your thoughts dictate your behavior; your behavior creates your character; change your heart- change your character!

A MIND-SET FOR CHANGE
DAY 28

When you allow your past to control your future you never operate in the present; the present is the starting line for your destination!

A MIND-SET FOR CHANGE
DAY 29

Success is not success without "U"!

A MIND-SET FOR CHANGE
DAY 30

You are your own best advocate; just for today, listen to yourself, compliment yourself, speak up for yourself, and do something for yourself; Your "self worth" will improve 50% overnight!

Preparing "The Plan"

What does a coach, an athlete, a teacher, a lawyer and a successful business owner have in common? – *a plan*!

Picasso states "our goals can only be reached through a vehicle of a plan, in which we must fervently believe, and upon which we must vigorously act. There is no other route to success."

Positive change requires a plan. When I considered changing to a healthy life-style, setting goals and deciding how to attain those goals were thought to be the most valuable advice I could give myself. Countless research has been conducted on behavior modification or changing behaviors. Studies show that "by setting personal goals to change behaviors and using learning strategies to achieve these, people can develop a greater sense of control and improve their health and well-being"(Hayes, 2010).

Remember, "*The Plan*" is only as good as the action you are willing to invest. According to health promotion officer Sally Hayes (2010), "brief interventions to help change unwanted behavior or lifestyle habits are effective in a range of settings." Whether the change you seek is healthy eating, starting an exercise program, or completing projects, *The Plan* is the key.

As you consider *The Plan,* you will also want to identify factors or barriers that can potentially inhibit or prevent the success of your plan. For example, I knew that purchasing sodas for my family members would increase the likelihood of my succumbing to the temptation. Sodas contain a fairly large amount of sugar which antagonizes my condition, Type II Diabetes. Therefore, I chose to eliminate it out of my diet completely.

> *Failure is inevitable where there is no plan to succeed!*
> *~ Rachel Spiller Riles*

In developing your plan you must, as Hayes (2010) suggest, consider the following psychological approaches to changing habits and behaviors: "1) learning to spot things that trigger or reinforce the unwanted behavior, 2) setting goals and planning how to achieve them, 3) building confidence to make important and wanted changes, 4) self-monitoring, 5) creating SMART action plans, 6) building social support through signposting, 7) rewarding success."(p. 21)

> *Insanity: doing the same thing over and over again and expecting different results.*
> *~Albert Einstein*

Sample Action Plan

Sample Action Plan

Complete the following. Choose goals you can commit to and invest the time.

Goals	Measures	Actions	Resources	Time
Lose 10 pounds	Pre and post weight using scale	1. Meal Plan – 1500 cal/day 1. Brisk Walking- 3 miles daily 2. No Fried Foods 3. No Sodas	1. $150.00 for meals, snacks 2. Proper walking shoes 3. Pedometer (app. for Iphone, Android)	Jan. 22, 2012 – February 21, 2012

Action Plan

Action Plan	Goals	Measures	Actions	Resources	Time

Bibliography

Aristotle. (n.d.). BrainyQuote.com. Retrieved May 1, 2013, from BrainyQuote.com Web site: http://www.brainyquote.com/quotes/quotes/a/aristotle145967.html

The Blue Letter Bible. (n.d.). *Blue Letter Bible.* Retrieved June 13, 2013, from http://www.blueletterbible.org

Cherry, K. (n.d.). *Stages of Change - How to Keep a Resolution.* Retrieved June 24, 2013, from http://psychology.about.com/od/behavioralpsychology/ss/behaviorchange.htm?p=1

Einstein, A.. (n.d.). BrainyQuote.com. Retrieved May 7, 2013, from BrainyQuote.com Web site: http://www.brainyquote.com/quotes/quotes/a/alberteins133991.html

Hayes, S. (2010). Brief interventions to change behavior. Practice Nurse. Retrieved June 24, 2013 from: http://www.healthpromcornwall.org/pdf/Brief%20Intervention%20Article%20in%20Practice%20Nurse%2026th%20March%202010.pdf

Lickerman, A. (2009, October 12). 5 Steps to changing any behavior. *Psychology Today*, Retrieved from http://www.psychologytoday.com/blog/happiness-in-world/200910/5-steps-changing-any-behavior

Maraboli, S. (2009). *Life, the Truth, and Being Free* . USA: Better Today Publishing.

Maxwell, J. C. (2009). *How successful people think, change your thinking, change your life*. Hachette Digital, Inc.

Patterson, A.L.(n.d.)Teaching methods for growth. Mt. Corinth M.B.Chuch, Houston, Texas.

Picasso. (n.d.). BrainyQuote.com. Retrieved May 1, 2013, from BrainyQuote.com Web site: http://www.brainyquote.com/quotes/quotes/p/pablopicas120939.html

President and Fellows of Harvard College. (2007, January). Why it's hard to change unhealthy behavior - and why you should keep trying. *Harvard Women's Health Watch*, Retrieved from http://www.health.harvard.edu.

Watson, J. B., & Kimble, G. (2007). *Behaviorism* (6th ed.). New Brunswick, U S A: Transaction Publishers. (Original work published 1924).

ABOUT THE AUTHOR

Rachel Spiller Riles, M.Ed

- An Author
- A Motivational Speaker
- An Educational Consultant
- A Continuing Professional Education (CPE) Provider for
- A Certified Educator, holding a Master of Arts in Education (Specialization—Curriculum & Instruction) Texas Education Agency
- A Master Registered Trainer (TECECDS—Texas Early Care and Education Career Development System)

She celebrates 31 years of marriage to Melvin. They have three children, Nashe', Taneisha, Melvin II and two grandchildren, Kadyn Emerie and McKenzie Audrielle.

www.ingramcontent.com/pod-product-compliance
Lightning Source LLC
Chambersburg PA
CBHW071311040426
42444CB00009B/1971